Published by Douglas King
@LoglinesRUs
www.LoglinesRUs.wordpress.com

Printed and bound in the United States of America

LOGLINES

The Long and Short on
Writing Strong Loglines

+ more than 250 sample loglines

Douglas King

Creator of @LoglinesRUS

Table of Contents

Introduction   1

    What is a Logline   3

    Evolution of a logline   7

Studio Loglines   11

Loglines

    Action/ Thriller   25

    Action/ Kung-Fu   41

    Animation   45

    Comedy   49

    Drama   83

    Found Footage   121

    Horror   125

    Romantic Comedy   133

    Sci-Fi/ Fantasy   145

    Thriller   153

    Television   157

Logline Laughs   163

INTRODUCTION

I launched the blog and Twitter account LoglinesRUs (www.loglinesrus.wordpress.com, @LoglinesRUs) in 2013 as a way to hone the craft of writing loglines and to test my ability to write, and publish, a logline every weekday. I wanted to provide a resource for other writers, producers and directors that might be seeking story ideas and offered the majority of the loglines for anyone to develop on their own without worry of copyright. With a few noted exceptions every logline was free for anyone to use and develop as they desired.

I also saw the benefit of the site as a promotional tool for my screenwriting. Over the course of the first year, I have enjoyed interacting with other writers discussing the craft of writing loglines as well as developing individual loglines I published with various producers.

After publishing over 200 original loglines I decided that collecting the majority of what I had published online into a printed book would make a handy desk reference that those in the film industry might enjoy. This is that product. Every logline presented in the main genre sections are free to be developed by anyone. Of course, if someone wished to have me write a detailed outline or the screenplay, I am available for such assignments.

The purpose of this book is twofold: to serve as a reference guide for writers who wish to perfect the art and craft of writing loglines, and to provide inspiration to those seeking content.

The importance of a strong logline cannot be underestimated and many times the logline is the only exposure a writer may have to producers, agents, and managers. If you only have one first impression—in this case only 35-40 words—it had better be great.

The loglines in this book are freely available as they are, or you may use them as a starting point for your own original story. Have fun. Mix and match. Change up genre and write your own stories. I would love to hear them. (Send them to me @LoglinesRUs.)

What follows is a discussion on what defines a logline and how to write one that will hopefully get you noticed. This is followed by an opening section where I have included a handful of loglines from popular films with which you may already be familiar, so you can get a feel for how the logline compares.

The genre categories include all of the original loglines published on LoglinesRUs. The final section, Logline Laughs, is filled with twisted and hopefully humorous loglines for well-known films to illustrate that, if you have a warped sense of humor, you can describe a film accurately but not with the same intent and context as the original filmmaker planned. These I include just for fun and because it is a good writing exercise (at least if you want to exercise you comedy muscle).

I listed the loglines into genre categories for easy reference. One reader may only be interested in Comedies, while another prefers Science Fiction, or Horror. Whatever your taste, there are bound to be a number of loglines that will entertain and hopefully inspire you.

Some loglines could easily fall into multiple genres and in some cases I have repeated a logline in a second genre where I felt it was important to note. I chose the primary genre to list a logline based on the most predominate theme and tone for the film as I intended when I wrote it.

Of course, the purpose of this book is to inspire you to create, so please feel free to take a logline you find here and switch genre or combine with another idea to create something wholly original.

What is a Logline?

A logline is defined as one sentence that provides enough information about the protagonist, antagonist, setting, genre, and story that the reader can fully grasp what the film will be. Daniel Manus, the founder of No Bullscript consulting service (www.nobullscript.net) says, "A logline will inherently get across a project's structure, hook, genre, tone, dilemma, major conflict, climax, and character arc." All in under 40 words!

Like the art of haiku, writing loglines is a skill that must be practiced and honed in order to compose well. For instance, writing a logline will cause you to focus on the utmost specifics and essence of your film without all the miscellaneous details. Writing a good logline will cause you to purely define the heart of your story and will help you in understanding what your theme and primary story is. This should help keep you focused as you sit down to write your screenplay. If you find yourself straying from the original logline, you need to carefully consider if you are deviating from the true heart of your story, or, if your logline correctly describes the film you wish to write.

Robert Kosberg, known as the Pitch King, is quoted as saying, "Screenwriters usually focus on the craft of screenwriting...plot, developing characters, but these all fall aside if the initial concept is not clear. Find great ideas. Keep asking yourself, Do you have a good idea here?"

I personally make writing the logline one of the first steps in outlining and preparing to write a script. I know if I can tell my story succinctly in 35 words, then I have a clear grasp of what the story, conflict, and theme are.

Screenwriters should also become proficient at writing loglines because the logline is what you will pitch to attract a potential producer, agent, manager. That's right. The 35 – 40 word sentence will be the determining factor as to whether your script will be read by a production company or languish on your computer's hard drive.

Let's talk specifics. What makes a good logline? Does it have a format?

Here is a list of the basics which all loglines must include:
The genre
Time period (if period piece)
Setting (if important)
The protagonist
Set up the inciting incident
The main conflict
What the protagonist must accomplish
What, or who, stands in their way from accomplishing goal?
The hook. What makes your story different?

A logline should illustrate that your story is an easily understood concept. The logline should be provocative. Would you want to see this movie based on this description? Would actors want to star in it? You must include character (protagonist and antagonist) plus conflict. What is the jeopardy? What is at stake?

A bad logline would be vague and discuss the theme and tone without giving any detail of the story itself. Never state the theme of the film. A logline should not include, "a deeply moving love story…" or any editorializing on the author's part. Focus on the concept and characters.

Would you want to read a screenplay based on this logline?

> "A wonderful heartfelt tale of love, loss, regret and ultimately reconciliation in Alabama."

No, but this might make you want to read more:

> "After leaving her redneck family to reinvent herself as a socialite in New York and becoming engaged to the mayor's son, a hard-working woman must return to Alabama to finalize her divorce where she learns a secret about her estranged husband."

This describes the film *Sweet Home Alabama* starring Reese Witherspoon, Josh Lucas and Patrick Dempsey. Which logline do you think better describes the film and could possibly get a producer's attention?

Ultimately the logline for your story should be unique but familiar. You want your story to grab the reader's attention but not be so different from anything they have read before that they cannot understand the story. Essentially, you want to show: when this happens, this person must (insert verb here) before (or else) this consequence occurs.

There are a few set rules to writing a logline. It must be only 35-45 words long. It must be only one sentence long. (Any longer and it becomes a synopsis. Any shorter and it becomes a tagline.)

There are also a few rules of thumb which will guide you to writing stronger loglines, but these are not hard and fast rules.

"The first few words of your logline should basically tell us what the general world of your screenplay is and what the inciting incident is that thrusts us (and your protagonist) into the story," describes Manus. "The first few words can also set up the stakes of the story."

Use active and action words, not passive words. Words such as "after," "when," or "as" are great to begin your logline followed by words such as "forces," "must," "discover," "uncover," "expose," "destroy," or "prevent," illustrate what happens to the protagonist and what must be accomplished. Then end with "before," "or else," to show what is at stake; the jeopardy.

For example:
    "<u>After</u> such and such…"
    "<u>When</u> such and such…"
    "…then (protagonist) is <u>forced</u>…"
    "…then (protagonist) <u>must discover</u>…"

The second portion of the logline tells the reader who your protagonist is and what they have to accomplish in the second and third act to achieve their goal. This is also the time to describe who opposes them and what is at stake (the jeopardy).

When preparing to write your logline, answer your questions about your film. If you can't, go directly to jail. Do not pass Go. Do not collect $200. While there, work on your film's outline until you can answer these questions.

Who is your main character?

What is he or she trying to accomplish?

Who is trying to stop him or her?

What happens if he or she fails?

Writing a strong logline is also a good time to flex your proverbial "verb" muscle. Use words that are visual and dynamic to describe your character and the scene. You have only 35 words - make every one count.

Use verbs such as "battle," "grapples," "jousts," "duels," "spars," "scraps," "clashes," in place of "fights," "opposes," and "contends with."

Your words should be exciting!

The logline should end with the jeopardy; what is at stake. Never give away the ending. You want the reader to want to know what happens. Leave them wanting more. After reading your logline, the desire should be so strong to know what happens to your characters that they can't wait to read the entire script.

But, do not write rhetorical questions as part of your logline. Never, ever, never. Did I mention never? This is not a logline:

"What would happen if you were a young boy tired of being small who wished to grow up and be big, and your wish came true?"

Instead,

"After making a wish at a fortune teller machine, a young boy becomes a grown man overnight and must cope with finding a place to live, finding a job, and adult relationships, with only the help of his ten year old friend." ~ *Big*

Here are more examples of good loglines from famous movies. Can you guess the film?

• A police chief, with a phobia for open water, battles a gigantic shark with an appetite for swimmers and boat captains in spite of a greedy town council who demands that the beach stay open. (35 words)

• A Parisian rat teams up with a wanna-be, no-talent chef, battling convention and the critics to prove that anyone can cook and open their own restaurant. (27 words)

• A lawyer who loses his ability to lie for 24 hours, clashes with his ex-wife for the affection of their son and the healing of their family. (26 words)

• A young farmer joins the rebellion to save his home planet from the evil empire when he discovers he is a warrior with legendary psychokinesis powers. (26 words)

Answers: *Jaws, Ratatouille, Liar, Liar,* and *Star Wars.*

Evolution of a Logline

I wanted to briefly illustrate the evolution of writing a logline. What follows is an example of the many drafts that might go into honing a strong logline that hopefully illustrates the difference between so-so and superb. I will also explain the reasons I made the various changes.

In this case, I was asked by a writer to critique and rewrite a logline for a script he is writing. The following logline is owned by Laughing Dragon Entertainment, LLC.

1st draft provided by writer: "A lonely science teacher dies and goes to summer camp, where he learns to connect with others and in the process alters the future of humanity." (26 words)

This is fine, but does not establish an inciting incident or conflict. We know who the protagonist is (the lonely science teacher). We know the setting (summer camp).

2nd draft: "When a lonely science teacher dies and goes to summer camp, he learns, with help from supernatural beings, how to connect with others, in the process altering the future of humanity." (31 words)

Better. I boosted the inciting incident (the death) and established that the story takes place after this event by beginning the logline with "When." This sets up the second act, but what about the third act?

We now know the protagonist is not alone (supernatural beings), which provides a sense of genre and we have an idea of the story (protagonist has to learn how to connect with others).

But there is still no sense of conflict or jeopardy.

3rd Draft: "When a lonely science teacher dies and wakes up in a campground, he must learn, with help from supernatural beings, how to connect with others before the Grim Reaper comes for him." (32 words)

All right. We are starting to get a sense of conflict, jeopardy and danger. The Grim Reaper is coming!

Final draft: "When a lonely science teacher dies and wakes up in a campground, he must learn, with help from supernatural beings, how to connect with others to alter the future of humanity before the Grim Reaper comes for him." (38 words)

In this final draft, I added back the phrase "to alter the future of humanity" to establish the stakes of the film. This elevates the tension and establishes a goal for our protagonist. This also creates a purpose for the story. If the teacher is dead, why does he care to connect to others or alter the future of humanity? This is why I added "must" (the imperative) and "the Grim Reaper" (the jeopardy). Now there is conflict and a goal. We have established the inciting incident, the second and third act.

Television Loglines

Writing a logline for a television show is a bit different than writing for film. The logline for a television show must illustrate how the story will be able to span multiple episodes and seasons and must include a larger hook and the world (or setting) in which the show will take place. You can write one logline for the pilot and another for the series. Less focus is placed on the character and more emphasis is made of the setting which allows for multiple stories to take place.

Television loglines may also include some details about the method by which it is produced, such as single-camera, or reference other films and shows.

> *Everybody Loves Raymond*
> A likeable husband's tolerance and marriage are tested by the constant intrusion of his overbearing parents and dim-witted brother.

The following are examples of loglines for pilots from the 2013-2014 season.

> *Trophy Wife*
> A reformed party girl finds herself with an instant family when she falls in love with a man who has three manipulative children and two judgmental ex-wives.

Mixology
A high-concept, single-camera comedy set in the world of a sexy Manhattan bar, chronicling the exploits of singles in search of love – all over the course of one night.

Almost Human
An action-packed buddy cop drama, set in the near future, when all LAPD officers are partnered with highly evolved human-like androids.

Sleepy Hollow
A modern-day supernatural thriller based on the legend of Sleepy Hollow.

Undateable
A young ensemble centering on a group of friends dubbed the "Undateables" whose lives are altered when a more confident character enters their world.

The Blacklist
The world's most wanted criminal mysteriously turns himself in and offers to give up everyone he has ever worked with on one condition: he will only work with a newly minted FBI agent with whom he seemingly has no connection.

Conclusion

Ironically, it takes longer to describe what a logline is and how to write a good one (1,867 words) than a logline is ever allowed to be.

Being able to write an outstanding logline is not only an art, but a sign of a true wordsmith. It shows potential buyers that you understand your story as well as the craft of screenwriting and can ply your trade professionally.

I hope you enjoy reading the following loglines. I don't

imagine this is a book you will pick up and read from cover to cover (although you could). Feel free to skip around, read only the genres you like, or read one a day as they were originally published. However you wish to utilize this resource I do hope you will be inspired to write your own loglines.

I would love to read them if you do and am available to critique and consult on loglines. I can be reached via my Twitter account @LoglinesRUs.

NOW SHOWING

STUDIO
LOGLINES

What follows are examples of published loglines for produced films with which you should be familiar. The purpose of including these in this book is to illustrate the art of logline using subjects you already know, so you can compare how well the logline describes the film.

3:10 To Yuma

A quiet rancher leads a posse on a dangerous mission to transport an outlaw to a town where a train will take him to prison.

Adjustment Bureau

A congressman falls in love with a woman and struggles against a supernatural organization determined to keep them apart.

American Graffiti

A couple of high school grads spend one final night cruising the strip with their buddies before they go off to college.

Argo

A CIA specialist concocts a covert operation to produce a fake Hollywood movie to rescue six American diplomats during the 1979 Iranian hostage crisis.

Armageddon

When an asteroid is headed for Earth, an elite blue-collar deep-core drilling team is sent to nuke the rock and save the world from Armageddon.

Bedtime Stories

After discovering the magical power of the bedtime tales that he spins for his nieces and nephew, a self-absorbed architect tries to manipulate this enchanted energy to his own advantage.

The Blair Witch Project

Three film students go missing after traveling into the woods of Maryland to make a documentary about the local Blair Witch legend leaving only their footage behind.

The Bourne Identity

A man with amnesia discovers he is a governmental assassin who has been targeted for death by the organization that employs him.

The Count of Monte Cristo

A sailor is wrongfully imprisoned for treason and escapes with plans to avenge those who accused him.

Charlotte's Web

A kindly spider helps a lone pig from being sent to the slaughter by turning him into a celebrity.

The Departed

A cop who's a mole and a mole who's a cop battle to decide the fate of a legendary Boston mobster.

Elf

When a thirty-year-old elf learns he is human, he leaves the North Pole to live with his birth father.

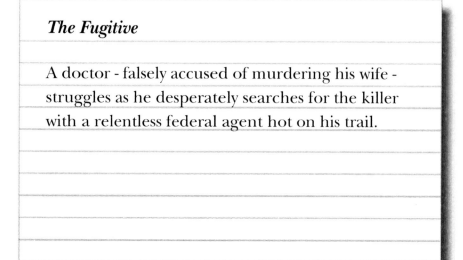

The Fugitive

A doctor - falsely accused of murdering his wife - struggles as he desperately searches for the killer with a relentless federal agent hot on his trail.

Little Miss Sunshine

A dysfunctional family takes a cross-country trip in their VW bus to get their seven-year-old daughter to the finals of a beauty pageant.

Lovely Bones

After her rape and murder, a teenage girl observes (from heaven) the aftermath of her demise and the continuation of life on earth.

Minority Report

In a future where criminals are arrested before the crime occurs, a despondent cop struggles on the lam to prove his innocence for a murder he has not yet committed.

Moneyball

After a disastrous season, the desperate General Manager of the Oakland A's uses a new-fangled statistical method to recruit three players to replace one.

Napoleon Dynamite

A listless and alienated teenager decides to help his new friend win the class presidency in their small western high school, while he must deal with his bizarre family life back home.

Rocky

A washed up boxer gets a chance to fight the world champ, but with the help of his lover, must learn to believe in himself before stepping into the ring.

Secretariat

A Denver housewife inherits her father's ranch and turns an unlikely horse into the record breaking, Triple Crown winning Secretariat.

Star Wars

Luke Skywalker, a spirited farm boy, joins rebel forces to save Princess Leia from the evil Darth Vader, and the galaxy from the Empire's planet-destroying Death Star.

Taken

An overprotective dad reveals his true colors – a black ops background - when his daughter is kidnapped in France, and he wreaks mayhem and murder to save her life.

Titanic

A young man and woman from different social classes fall in love aboard the ill-fated voyage of the Titanic.

ACTION/ THRILLER

The Action / Thriller category can be an all encompassing description for a dramatic film with action elements (i.e. large stunt set pieces such as shooting, explosions, car chases, etc.) and additional story elements of mystery and intrigue.

Other genre films also fall into this category including war, supernatural, science fiction, fantasy, espionage, western, and crime.

For the sake of simplicity, I have included loglines that may fall into the aforementioned sub-genres within the Action / Thriller category.

The Cave

Upon discovering that a distress signal is a rouse to lure unsuspecting ships into a deadly trap, the crew of a fishing trawler must fight for their lives to escape a crazed clan of cannibals.

Masterful

After finding his wife dead in her art studio, a man must unravel a conspiracy of international art forgery, involving the women he thought he knew, before he and his son are murdered too.

The God Complex

When a cloning experiment by genetic scientist goes horribly wrong, the military sends their best man to clean up and avert an international crisis.

Deadly Pillow Talk

When a hitman, who talks in his sleep, confesses to multiple murders to a hooker with a big mouth, he must evade both the mob boss that hired him and the police, if he wants to live.

Undiscovered

Upon entering a secluded cenote in Central America, a team of scientists discover they have disturbed the feeding grounds of a prehistoric creature.

Drones

The skies are filled with malfunctioning, autonomous killer drones and mankind has move underground to survive until one teen decides to fight back.

Baja

When a father and son novice racing team decides to enter the Baja 500 they face challenges to survive not only the race but drug dealers and corrupt Mexican military.

Blackhats

When the NSA director admits to domestic spying then solicits the aid of the best hackers, a small band of hackers decide to fight what they feel is wrong only to be entwined in an international terrorist threat and discover their initial instincts were wrong.

Bilderburg

When the secret annual meeting of the world's
most powerful CEOs and politicians is taken
hostage by international terrorists, an elite team
responds to rescue them while the entire situation
is hidden from the public.

Eze

When spiritual forces of darkness ascend to wreck
havoc in West Texas, only a grizzled Harley riding
ex-preacher can battle them to save mankind.

MERCS

The years take their toll on five South African high school mates hired as mercenaries to fight across the Dark Continent.

Finishing School

After completing BUDS, the men trying to become Navy Seals must complete a year long program before conducting their first real world mission and ultimately receiving the Trident.

Harmony

After her brother is gunned down by a notorious
Hispanic gang, a young woman grows up to
become an undercover detective and infiltrates
the deadly gang to bring them to justice.

Monsoon

During the worst rainy season to hit Vietnam
in decades, a war vet vacationing with his wife
faces a new life and death challenge against the
environment.

Road Kill

A couple traveling cross-country encounter
problems from police and suspicious locals when
they are accused of a fatal hit and run accident
and must prove their innocence, or die trying.

On your Six

A Special Forces team is sent on a mission to
evacuate the embassy staff in a war-torn African
country when all hell breaks loose and they must
"exfil" across militia filled country-side while being
pursued by a maniacal warlord.

Off Book

When his handler at the CIA turns up murdered, a covert operative, who has been working on unsanctioned missions, must erase his own existence when he suddenly finds himself the target of not only his enemy but his own country.

Hunter, Gatherer

An anal-retentive analyst and an operator are forced to work together, using their respective skills and talents, to evade the enemy all around them while trying to escape a hostile country when their field office is destroyed and everyone murdered.

Na Pali

When a freak storm forces a tourist kayaking adventure on the Na Pali coast to beach, the vacationing couples and guides are in greater danger from drug dealers protecting their secret crops.

Slide

After a devastating mudslide destroys a small town, the captain of the volunteer fire department gathers the remaining citizens to help find not only the missing but his own family.

45 Ways to Die

When a hit man decides to retire, he finds he must defend his life from every other professional assassin, and a few aspiring to be, who try to kill him to make a name for themselves.

Allen Station

Sam Bass and his notorious band of outlaws plan and execute the historic first train robbery in Allen, Texas, only to be tracked and hunted by Texas Rangers to Round Rock, where the gang is staging a bank robbery.

Hush

When a detective partners with parents of an abducted child cold-case to investigate a recent abduction, he uncovers a mystery that could result in solving both crimes.

Death Pays All Debts

When an abusive husband goes to prison for the murder of his wife, he later learns that she staged her own death in retribution for years of abuse.

Briggs

A successful bodyguard for celebrities is challenged when a serial stalker focuses on destroying him by way of attacking his clients and he must stop the fanatic before one of his clients is murdered.

Light it Up

When a special force squad engages a handful of militants on the Afghanistan-Pakistan border, a hornet's nest is opened after the squad discovers an enormous tunnel system and weapons cache protected by two divisions of battle hardened warriors.

Too Far

When their village in Darfur is attacked by radical Muslims, a family risks their lives to escape by crossing a vast desert alone, pursued by militants, in hopes of reaching safety in Chad.

Calatrava Cross

After the execution of the last Knights Templar, an order of Spanish Knights of the Calatrava Cross must hide from the government and the attacking Moors who wish to uncover their secrets and power.

Burn it Down

When the mayor of Chicago decides to crack down on crime he faces an organized army of various crime syndicates who have banded together, so he calls in a private army to deal with the problem.

Wurmz

A small mid-western town is terrorized by parasitic worms that bubble up from the local quarry swimming hole.

ACTION/ KUNG-FU

A sub-set of Action is Kung-Fu, or martial arts films. I separated these films into their own category due to the specific focus of the action on the fighting as opposed to general action of car chases and war.

Kung-Fu films were very popular in the 1970s thanks to the brilliant martial artist Bruce Lee. Chuck Norris continued the tradition in many films but his films often included additional action elements of war. Steven Segal, Jean-Claude Van Damme and Jackie Chan also produced many great Martial Art films.

A resurrection of the genre occurred in 2000 with the release of *Crouching Tiger, Hidden Dragon* which ushered in a new style of Kung-Fu film, one where actors on wires performed ever more spectacular fight sequences.

A Man and His Monkey

A wandering warrior poet, who travels with a pet monkey, decides to protect a young widow he encounters, from a criminal clan that has targeted her because of her beauty.

3 Rings

When the annual contest for the best multi-discipline fighter is announced, the feudal village hosting the event is filled with heroes and criminals and one local is challenged to save the honor of his family and betrothed wife.

Blade of Grass

When invaders attack a defenseless farming village, one farmer, with hidden and forbidden fighting skills, must decide to reveal his secret and save the village he loves or hide his skills to avoid punishment from the emperor.

Six-pack Chopra

A new-age guru is also a kung-fu master who must battle an evil society when he uncovers their plot to control society through pop culture and music, culminating in showdown at a hypnotic three-day rock festival.

Pounding Flesh

After his girlfriend is murdered in the cross-fire between two rival gangs, one man trains to enact revenge a pound of flesh at a time, taking on both gangs single-handedly.

ANIMATION

Walt Disney made the animated feature film famous. Pixar made it a multi-billion dollar business.

Animated films are as much for adults as children. The bright colors and silly talking animals amuse children while the sometimes sophisticated puns, asides, and sight gags may go over the head of the youngest viewer, but are enjoyed by adults who are really kids at heart.

Storylines are becoming more mature for animated films and Japanese animated films deal with very adult themes and plots.

The Last Whale

A young whale left to fend for himself after his parents are killed by whalers embarks on a journey of discovery.

Swarm

The class struggle between ground bugs and flying bugs culminates in a world war.

Tiki Tiki

When a volcano on a tiny Pacific island awakens and threatens to destroy the entire island, it falls to one parrot and his lemur friend to save the other creatures and get them off the island.

COMEDY

I love comedy. I love to laugh. So, this section may be a bit long. Within the Comedy category there are a few film ideas that cross over into Action, Fantasy and Drama.

The first question one might ask is, "how can a comedy also be a drama?" Films such as *The Wolf of Wall Street* fit that category. It is very much a drama but some of the situations and dialog are very comedic. Then there are films which can be defined as a Comedy with Action elements such car chases, gun fights and explosions. Many of these films also have very a dramatic theme to them. *We're the Millers* comes to mind.

Comedy also comes in many forms: situational, absurd, romantic (see Romantic Comedy section), dark, blue (or raunchy) spoof/ satire, and more.

The Rooster

After learning their high school's most popular student is in trouble, a group of friends discover, through reminiscing, that the student wasn't as bad as they remembered and they team together to save him.

To Be Young Again

When the wish of a 40 year old man to relive his youth knowing now all he does now comes true, he discovers life is not as easy as he had thought.

Big in reverse.

The Tell

When an up and coming poker player gets burned by a beautiful women connected to organized crime, he regains his status with the help of a mystical old mentor to challenge her in the World Series of Poker.

Pitchmen

Up and coming ad execs by day, club going playboys at night; five friends drink, dance and screw their way through Chicago until one mistakenly sleeps with their firm's biggest client.

Stop and Rob

The slacker staff at a corner convenience store must toughen up to fight off a gang of thugs who nightly rob the place and commit violence, or lose all respect in the neighborhood and their jobs.

Nutted

The week before his wedding, the groom gets a swift kick in the nuts causing him to see his girlfriend's baby as a grown man in a onesie who guides him and tests him on his readiness for marriage and fatherhood.

Devil Pups

A group of teens enter a summer camp sponsored by the Marine Corps at Camp Pendleton where they discover their own mental and physical strength while trying to stay out of trouble.

Stripes meets *Stand by Me.*

Daydream Believer

When a young boy would rather live in his day dreams than face the harsh truth of his bullied school boy existence, his teacher and parents must rescue him before he is lost forever.

Characters from the Bowels of My Mind

When an author encounters the characters he writes in the real world, creating a number of awkward and humorous moments, he must help them assimilate or return to the stories they belong in.

The Existential Experiences of Mark & Sneed

Best friends journey together on a magical, hallucinogenic voyage that may or may not really be happening on the summer after they graduate from college and have to face the seriousness of adult life.

Tarantino's Final Cut

When Quentin Tarantino mysteriously dies with
an unseen, unproduced screenplay, the blood
and guts start flying as Hollywood eviscerates itself
when those in the industry turn on each other to
be the ones to star in, produce and direct the film.

Mail Room

Friends working in the mail room of a talent
agency in Hollywood decide to get revenge on the
evil agents who make their lives hell.

Office Space and *Horrible Bosses* meets *Entourage*

I Need to Meet Anna Kendrick or I'll Die

When a young man feels the only path to happiness is to meet Anna Kendrick, the woman of his dreams, he sets out to do anything possible to meet her.

Buck Wild

Friends working in a hedge fund trade all day and tear it up all night until the market crashes and they are out of jobs.

The Hangover meets *Wall St.*

Party City

When a couple of friends go out for a night on the town, nothing could prepare them for the chaos of a string of unfortunate events which take place and which they must overcome to stay out of jail and stay alive.

Baked

Two stoners hide their stash in baked goods before an impending police raid, only to have those baked goods mistakenly entered into a contest, where they win a contract with a national distributor, launching a successful new brand, which the police are investigating.

The Joint

A mythical marijuana joint with magical powers prompts a stoner and his friend to go on a quest to protect and discover its origins while avoiding the police and a rival drug dealer who wishes to use the doobie in a nefarious plot.

Gil

A quirky young man, with an incredible talent for sketching, creates a wondrous world for him and his friends to explore to escape the banality of prep school and a restrictive headmaster.

Naked and Famous

After a photo of four, naked, pot-smoking friends accidently gets posted online and goes viral, the group face fame and fortune which threatens to tear their friendship apart when egos and favoritism arise.

Cat & Mouse

When two competitive friends grow up on opposite sides of the law they are entangled in a cat and mouse game until they are forced to partner to solve a string of crimes before one, or both, are killed.

Lifer

After a young man realizes he must follow in his father's footsteps of owning a fourth-generation pub in Dublin, his ideas of modernization put him at odds with his family and the townsfolk which starts a village-wide conflict.

Banal

A sarcastic, angry loner, who distrusts and dislikes everyone, is confronted with a vibrant, fun loving personal assistant who changes his attitude over one summer when she takes care of him after he suffers a stroke.

Sexy Misbehavior

Two smart and powerful female lingerie designers
make a bet to see who can sleep with the goody-
two-shoes intern first, only to discover it is much
more difficult than they thought and ultimately
puts their careers at risk.

The Fluffers

When an aspiring actor and actress meet traveling
to Los Angeles to pursue their dreams, their
decade's long friendship helps them through
the lean years as "on set assistants" in the adult
industry, through jealousy and up to their break in
film.

When Harry Met Sally meets *Boogie Nights*

The Review

A film director takes drastic measures for 24-hours to avoid reading or hearing the review of his latest "masterpiece" which he feels could make or break his career.

Dead-ends

Five friends, each struggling with career, finances and relationships, meet weekly for dinner and drinks where they swap stories and give each other bad advice, in this slice of life film.

G

A writer and photographer covering a political sex scandal concerning the secret service, become embroiled in danger and intrigue when their gonzo behavior draws them in to the very story they are covering.

The Hangover meets *All the President's Men.*

Earned Distrust

When one of a three-man con-artist team decides to go legit after he finds the woman of his dreams, his friends devise a con forcing him to return to his criminal ways or be exposed for who he really is.

Daft

After two bumbling idiots lose their menial jobs,
they set out on a cross country journey of self
discovery and pub crawls, only to find themselves
the focus of a news feature which suddenly makes
them local celebrities.

Puck Fair

When King Puck, a goat, is stolen the eve before
the Puck Fair in Killorglin, Ireland, the village
is thrown into a wild mele of accusations and
generational family feuds to solve the mystery of
the missing billy before the big day.

Snark

As a syndicated columnist reaches the end of
an illustrious career his family plans a large
retirement party which he bemoans and frets over
until his estranged daughter returns home to
celebrate with him.

Plump Women Need not Apply

A successful misogynistic business man advertises
for a wife with very specific requirements, only to
find his checklist shattered when he falls in love
with a woman who does not meet his deal-breaking
desires.

Roadie

An aging roadie, with no family, is near the end of his usefulness, when the band he has worked for his entire career announces their retirement, and he must convince others he can still handle the job or risk forced retirement and loneliness.

Bait & Switch

A team of beautiful con artists work Las Vegas when a competing group of con-men encroach on their action and they must all decide to work together, undermine each other, or both, to stay one step ahead of their marks and the police.

PS

On the eve of their 60th wedding anniversary, a couple decides to renew their vows and have a second honeymoon which causes some concern amongst their children, grand children and great grandchildren.

FYI

When an upstart Internet streaming video site promotes its launch with an announcement that it will be live broadcasting the coming Biblical apocalypse, all Hell breaks loose, literally, and the employees are the only ones prepares to deal with the aftermath.

Gorilla

A young brother and sister must come to terms
and deal with a new demanding and over-bearing
step-father who their mother surprises them with
after her weekend in Vegas.

Revue

A manic depressive director with ADD attempts
to stage a revue including all of his favorite
things while dealing with a prima donna actor,
an insecure actress, temperamental writers and
stressed out producers.

Whiskey & Rye

Two competing families of distiller in Ireland compete for who can make the finest whiskey and win an international competition.

Palm Days

The summer vacation before college means four things for a group of friends: Destin Beach, a two man volley ball tournament, drinking and a summer fling.

It's in your Head

When a senior executive for a major Hollywood studio suffers a nervous breakdown over the summer tent-pole releases, he is admitted into a mental institute where his film-like fantasies have a profound effect on the other patients and he discovers the next big hit.

Peg Legs

A misfit band of pirates that no captain will take as crew, stumble upon what they believe is a map to great riches and secretly attempt to recover the treasure themselves without the other pirate crews discovering their plot.

Pulp

After reaching the milestone of having published 100 pulp fiction paperback novels, the author decides it is time to retire only to discover the characters from his novels don't want him to as each begins appearing in the flesh to persuade him to keep writing.

Palms

When a grifter travels to the Cayman Islands to take advantage of the tourists at the resorts, the last thing he expected was to become a hero after a hurricane forces him to use his skills and talents to help others recover from the disaster.

Master Debater

After being downsized from his sales job, one man must find work to save his marriage so he hires himself out as a debater, only to find a rival in his former a-hole boss who was also fired.

Duds

Three slackers are each evicted from their parent's basements and must face adulthood, responsibility and maturity with each other's help if they are to survive.

Ink

In order to avoid cancelation, a graphic novel artist draws himself into his book and becomes entwined in the story, where he fights the villains, falls in love with the heroine and realizes his hero is a dick.

Planet Crazy

After a mad scientist introduces a chemical into the world's drinking water, causing everyone to go insane, one couple, who spent a wild weekend together in a secluded mountain cabin, must find a cure to save all of humanity.

High Tide

Imminent rising water levels threaten the tiny island Republic of Kiribati and a team from the Peace Corps must assist the reluctant islanders to relocate to a safer location before it is too late.

WTF

One successful business woman must reverse a voodoo curse, placed on her by a bitter rival, which causes her to experience the worst of Murphy's Law during one hellacious week.

The List

After waking up from a serious car accident, a woman writes a list of things she wants to change, but in other people not herself, and she makes everyone angry when she attempts to "fix" them so she can be happy.

The Reluctant Messiah

After a YouTube video is posted of a man waxing philosophically on a beach in Carmel, California, he becomes a reluctant guru, when people flock to him seeking guidance and wisdom for their lives.

Opus

A writer tries to salvage his sanity by purging his mind of every last creative thought into one magnum opus only to find resistance from his publisher and wife who want him to keep writing more books even if it kills him.

Prom King

When his high school best friend appears the day he is laid-off from work and dumped by his girlfriend, one man gets swept up in nostalgia and starts behaving like the prom king he was, only to discover that doesn't help a man in his thirties.

Rollers

Four friends visit Las Vegas and their friendship is tested when one friend hits a multi-million dollar jackpot, another is caught cheating the casino, another cheating on his wife, and another considering an impromptu wedding.

Head Shots

When two hairstylist open a salon to pamper the rich and famous of Beverly Hills they are unprepared for the drama and extreme expectations placed on them by their clients or the cut-throat competition from their former boss.

The Most Ignored Man on Earth

When one man reaches his limit of being
ignored by everyone on social media and in real
life, including his own family and dog, he takes
extreme measures to become noticed.

Connections

A lonely woman, seeking any type of connection
with another human, places an ad in a newspaper
for friends and is shocked by the responses and
realizes she is not alone.

Beat Offs

When his garage band breaks up after 20 years, an over-40 drummer seeks fame by traveling to Los Angeles to compete in an international drum competition where he finds unfriendly rivals, supportive sponsors and even more supportive groupies.

Chill

A laid-back family in Hawaii has their world turned upside-down when a "cousin" from the mainland visits, bringing all of her worldly possessions including emotional baggage and each must influence the other to achieve a balanced life.

F**K

After being mentioned as an influence by a famous hip-hop artist, an aging, retro, funkadelic band tries to regain its illustrious stature by staging a comeback concert in a run-down theater in Minneapolis.

1,000 Legs

After an exterminator stumbles upon a nest of centipedes and is eaten to the bone, the small town of Paia, Maui fights back, lead Afghanistan war vet, against the creepers who are terrorizing and taking over their town.

Anal Worms

When a parasite infected hitchhiker dies in a small town, the sheriff must save the residents from the plague or worms that burrow into the human body and eat it from the inside out.

Die! Die! Die!

When a family moves into a rural home, the father, who suffers from arachnophobia, discovers the basement is a nest to thousands of spiders who fight him for control of the home.

DRAMA

Drama is possibly the largest category because most films, regardless of their genre, are dramatic in nature. Even films with comedy can also be considered a drama as previously noted.

Science Fiction and Fantasy films can be considered dramatic. *The Hobbit,* which is obviously a high-concept fantasy film, is also a Drama, and would also fall under action with its huge action set pieces.

In this section, I have included all the films I consider Dramas regardless of their additional sub-genres. Some loglines may be repeated under other sections when it was important to note the strong elements present in that particular category.

Daddy & I

A precocious nine year old launches a vlog to express her feelings about her parent's divorce and her limited visitations with her dad, only to garner national attention and a world-wide audience.

The Epistemist

A young man, struggling to find his way in life, encounters a reclusive former professor, and discovers a new way of experiencing life to its fullest.

F**cked Up

A narcissistic sociopath with Napoleonic-complex, tries his best not to destroy everyone's life around him until he meets the love of his life and then the two become hell-bent on destroying the world.

Prodigal

When a playboy, slacker younger brother returns to join his father's growing corporate empire, tensions mount between his toe-the-line older sibling over who is better suited to run the company.

Shaman

Facing the stress of career, marriage and family, a man flees to the desert of Mexico where he encounters a wizened, tribal guide who shares wisdom and peyote setting the man on the path of happiness and enlightenment.

True North

After surviving two tours in Iraq, a young soldier returns home only to be thrust into a commanding role to help his family as they face the death of their father, a struggling economy and a wayward younger sister.

The Journeyman

A young man on the path to enlightenment travels the world and discovers love and life.

Lesser Degree

Legal interns, lead by a cocky maverick, are out of their depth when they manipulate themselves onto the case of a friend who has been accused of first degree murder.

Dream Maker

One man spends decades making the dreams of others come true in the entertainment industry even at the expense of his own family and dreams.

Homeless is Where is Heart Is

A homeless man with a philanthropic attitude affects his community with the results bringing change beyond the neighborhood.

99 to 1

Four separate and dissimilar families face the nation's economic challenges differently based on their status culminating in interconnected stories.

Tiny Dancer

An aspiring ballet dancer must overcome physical limitations and emotional heartbreak to become a professional dancer in New York's premier dance company.

Harboring Secrets

After a powerful Fortune 500 executive wakes up from an alcohol induced black-out, he finds his professional and personal secrets on the verge of being exposed which he must stop before his life, and that of the ones he loves is ruined.

Decompress

When a middle-aged, divorced father is downsized from the career he has had for decades, he retreats to a beach rental for solace to think about his future only to be interrupted by a couple who love to drink and a sexy local bartender.

This is Libby

A reclusive twenty-something who hides at her job in a boutique bookstore is reluctantly drawn into the real world of people, places and a possible relationship, by her brother who cares for her and wants to see her happy.

Zen and the Art of Lawn Care

After hiring an eccentric gardener to care for the dilapidated gardens of her estate, a widow discovers that his meticulous care is restoring more than just the flora, and her heart blooms as well.

Trafficking

A police detective tries to stop one of the largest sex traffic rings in Dallas run by a sadistic, female immigrant while he also covers up his own dark sexual addition.

Frame up

A good cop, who has been diagnosed with terminal cancer, devises a last ditch effort to arrest a career criminal by framing him for his murder when he kills himself and makes his death look like the criminal did it.

The Confessions

The weeks following the trial, crucifixion and resurrection of Jesus Christ, those involved must report to their superiors the events which happened.

Yes Virginia, There is a God

When a young girl shares with her mother's boyfriend that she does not believe in God, he leads them both on a journey of spiritual awakening.

The Long Con

A successful business executive of a multi-national bank realizes that his wife has been playing him for years as a part of a confidence scheme, and he must stop her before the final step which will make him look guilty for numerous federal crimes.

These are the Days of our Lives

Seven friends from high school have an impromptu reunion to reminisce and reflect on where their lives are headed.

Big Chill for Gen Y.

Headliner

A young Jewish woman must overcome family troubles when her orthodox father forbids her from pursuing a career as a pop star in the sometimes corrupt and always over-sexualized music industry.

Main St.

After a corporate store opens in small-town Middle America, one Main Street shop owner, set at odds with her husband who works for the big box store, must rally the other shop keepers to fight for their life-style and livelihood.

Let the Dead Bury the Dead

After a man receives the death penalty for the murder of his wife, he discovers once in jail that she framed him and is still alive and he must prove his innocence with the help of a lifelong friend to save his life.

Detox

When a young man enters rehab to get clean from years of narcotic use, he struggles to differentiate between reality and flashbacks, only to discover, with the aid of another addict, that there may be something sinister going on in the facility.

Paul who was Saul

After his road to Damascus conversion to faith in Christ, Paul becomes an apostle and preaches the gospel through-out the known world against the wishes of many.

Lincoln's Odyssey

After a penny is freshly minted it is passed from owner to owner in this slice of life, multi-generational journey.

Felt Jungle

After a nasty divorce, leaving her in debt, a woman struggles to keep her kids out of trouble and at home while working a new job as a black jack dealer in a Las Vegas casino.

Shadow Casting

A female intelligence agent sent to recruit assets in an Eastern European country on the brink of social-economic collapse finds herself conflicted when she begins working with one member of the protesting group and a member of the government.

Mud, Sweat and Tears

When a group of physically challenged youth
want to compete in a mud run, one man, with
emotional struggles of his own, steps up to help
them train and attempt to achieve their goal.

Tripping Through Acrylic

An artist takes a journey inside his own paintings
to recover his lost love but encounters resistance
from some of his painted subjects who want him
all to themselves.

Surf Texas

During the surfing and beach blanket bingo craze
of 1965, four friends from Dallas venture on a
road trip to Galveston in pursuit of cool waves and
hot babes.

Sugar Water

When sugar plantation owners of the Big Island of
Hawaii need to move their crops from the fields
to the coast for transportation to market, one
man engineers and oversees the construction of
an incredible network of water flumes through
mountains and valleys.

Dropping

The mercurial owner of an emerging indie record label struggles to keep the business going until his assistant, who has a crush on him, introduces him to a band that practices in her apartment building, which has huge potential.

30 Karat

When an international diamond dealer traveling to South America carrying a set of twelve 30 karat diamonds is robbed, he attempts to recover the diamonds while also being investigated for his possible role in the theft.

Close Out

Two bothers growing up in the beachside town of Encinitas compete for the same waves, girl and sponsors, but when one suffers a career ending injury and the other goes international, their relationship hits the reef.

Set in His Ways

A middle-aged single man, who has never been married, needs his friends help after he begins a relationship with a woman and his stubbornness against changing his familiar lifestyle could ruin everything.

Music of the Stars

A young girl, whose father dies in a space shuttle accident and whose mother is a relapsed alcoholic, finds solace in a planetarium where she believes her father speaks to her, providing her wisdom and insight, beyond her years, on how to deal with life's problems.

Shots

When a female bartender enters a screenwriting contest and her script makes the top three, suddenly her life goes from serving to being served, but her hard partying boyfriend feels left behind and threatens to expose a deep secret which could ruin everything.

Caught Inside

With news of an upcoming swell that could produce the largest most deadly waves in the world, one man, a legend of big wave surfing, must decide whether to make history, or keep a promise to his wife to never risk his life again.

Star Shower

When a spectacular, but unexplained, shower of shooting stars fills the daylight sky over a small West Texas town, the pastor must deal with a series of supernatural occurrences and fears that arise within the town.

Stoneface

After the death of his wife, a father, who has always been emotionally closed-off, must deal with his grief while also creating a nurturing home environment for his kids, with help from his brother and sister-in-law.

Hallucination

After his wife leaves him due to his slipping grasp of reality caused by consuming mass quantities of hallucinogenic drugs, one man, with the help of his teenage daughter, attempts to return to reality and save his life and marriage.

Dropping In

Three friends take one year to tour the world searching for the biggest waves to surf but face greater challenges in their relationships when rivalries and women come between them, pushing them to make life or death decisions.

Little Monkey Boy

After losing his father in a car accident, a young impressionable boy begins acting like a monkey, which his father affectionately nicknamed him, and his mother seeks help from a professional counselor.

Unrequited

Another attraction and another rejection face one man who must deal with a string of unrequited feelings throughout his life until he discovers that he has been on the opposite side of attraction in one of his closest friendships.

Chapter & Verse

When God stops answering prayer at a small town, a pastor takes drastic measures by forcing a lock-in with some of his congregation, until God will answer them.

And then...

When a retired widower grandfather decides to go on a singles cruise where he hopes to have one last hoorah, all but one grandchild who conspires with him, are worried and try to stop him.

Spring Water

When a young, lively professor joins the staff of a staid college campus he brings a fresh, rejuvenating perspective to life, education and relationships for the students and faculty.

Fuzzy Dice & Salsa

When a young Chicano male meets up with a beautiful cultured Salsa dancer two dissimilar worlds collide to form one incredible dance duo.

Willie and Abel

After Hurricane Katrina, two friends must work together, facing bureaucratic red-tape, lack of money, and local thugs, to rebuild not only their lives but the jazz club they owned on Bourbon Street in New Orleans.

Watch the World Die

When a coming apocalypse is reported by the news, one extremely intelligent but emotionally detached man prepares his resistant family to move to a special secret location where he plans to live in safety.

Hammerhead

After one of his children dies from alcoholism, a stubborn abusive father attempts to make amends to his estranged children.

Dead Blue

A homicide detective must catch a killer targeting police officers before his younger brother, who just graduated from the academy, becomes the next target.

Bucket Head

When a young man is relentlessly harassed in high school, he counters the cyber-bullying with fictitious posts from a gorgeous girlfriend and celebrity fans, suddenly becoming the school stud until his arch nemesis learns the truth.

Bar Backs

Two friends become bar-backs in the hippest, busiest bar in New York and encounter more nightlife than they can handle between the staff and the customers, which leads to friction between them when one excels faster in the job.

Deep Blue

Friends vacationing at the great blue hole off the coast of Belize, experience a profound, life-changing event and must deal with the ramifications after one dive to the very heart of the sinkhole.

Melt

A teenage runaway takes up with a crowd of MDMA eating, rave hoppers until her grasp of reality slips and she discovers dark secrets about her new friends so she must reach out to her father to rescue her.

TBH

When a teen girl begins dating a rebellious young man, her friends are forced to be honest about her new destructive behavior before it ruins her life including the aspiration she always had to go to a fine college.

To Start Being

When a group of strangers meet at a support group for people who have experienced traumatic events in their lives, they become friends and lean on each other for recovery and restoration forming emotional and romantic bonds.

Interment

When the US government places citizens into internment camps for disagreeing with policy, one man rallies fellow camp-mates to escape and destroy the camps, with help from their families, before more people are falsely imprisoned.

Civil Disturbance

After a radical president sends the armed forces
to round up political opponents that do not agree
with his policies one Texas town decides to fight
back to protect freedom, liberty and justice.

Sunken City

When spelunkers of a cenote in South America
find an ancient civilization once thought extinct,
they soon realize the discovery is unwelcomed and
dangerous.

The Beautiful Things

In the future art is considered a crime by the government and one man sets out to collect and store digital copies of all forms of art before they can be destroyed.

6th Street

A couple trying to make a living with their music in Austin, Texas, face challenges to their relationship and their artistic style when a producer takes a liking to not only their music but the female of the duo.

Falling off Monsters

When two extreme kayakers venture to Guatemala to traverse the challenging Rio Cahabon with its many 50-foot waterfalls, they encounter not only the dangers of the water but wildlife, the locals and drug cartels.

Just Be

After he finds enlightenment, one man tries to teach his uptight family how to relax and just be in each moment.

Private Army

When the world's governments turn to private armies, the balance of power shifts and one man, running a corporate army, discovers a plot to overthrow these very same governments and must act to stop a global military coup d'etat.

The Aerialist

One woman, suffering from bi-polar disorder, decides to forgo medical treatment with help from a homeopathic doctor, so she can live her life without the debilitating effects of drugs much to the displeasure of her family.

RC Pilot

A lonely man in Minnesota builds and flies RC planes until he makes a new friend where he works who begins to show him other pleasures in life including beer and women.

The All-Seeing

In the future a religious cult has taken over the government but one man, tired of being told what to do, fights back to restore personal freedom and individuality.

Room 10

When a woman finds a key in her dying father's possessions to a room in a seedy, downtown hotel, her life spirals out of control when she discovers her father had a dark secret past.

Turntables

In the competitive New York City nightclub scene, rival DJs battle on the dance floors and in their personal lives for success, both financial and in relationships.

FOUND FOOTAGE

This is a relatively new genre, thanks to the producers of *The Blair Witch Project*. Found Footage is defined by a cinematography style which mimics film as captured by a cell phone, hand-held video camera or other consumer recording device. The footage is almost always first person POV, with the exception of security camera footage as was used almost exclusively in the *Paranormal Activity* films. The events in the film occur without editing for the purpose of recording those events as they happen.

For some reason, the majority of found footage films also fall into the Horror, Thriller, Supernatural category. It would be really interesting to see this genre opened up to include Comedy or Martial Arts.

Wurmz

A small mid-western town is terrorized by parasitic worms that bubble up from the local quarry swimming hole.

Mop Up

The residual effect of a toxic spill is discovered to the horror and indiscriminate termination of the clean-up crew.

It's in the Sand

A hedonistic weekend turns deadly when friends at a luxury beach resort on a remote island discover deadly creatures under the beach sand which feast on blood.

NOW SHOWING

HORROR

Horror films have been around since the classic black and white monster movies produced by Universal Pictures. Today, Horror films fall into sub-categories of Slasher films (*Friday the 13th*, *Nightmare on Elm Street*), Torture Porn (*Saw*), Supernatural (*The Conjuring*, *The Ring*), and Found Footage (*Paranormal Activity*).

Horror films can also fall under Thrillers and vice-versa.

It Came from the Drain

An epidemic of mutant creatures attack
unsuspecting victims while in the bathroom
causing the mayor to call for federal help to save
the city.

Don't Blink

When people start mysteriously disappearing
in the blink of an eye after an electrical storm,
a group of teenagers struggle to find safety and
discover the reason for the disappearance before
they are all taken.

Blood Runner

Contestants in a mud run must compete for their lives when the organizers accidentally set up the course on the land of a sociopath, homicidal murder.

It's in the Sand

A hedonistic weekend turns deadly when friends at a luxury beach resort on a remote island discover deadly creatures under the beach sand which feast on blood.

Anal Worms

When a parasite infected hitchhiker dies in a small town, the sheriff must save the residents from the plague or worms that burrow into the human body and eat it from the inside out.

Die! Die! Die!

When a family moves into a rural home, the father, who suffers from arachnophobia, discovers the basement is a nest to thousands of spiders who fight him for control of the home.

1,000 Legs

After an exterminator stumbles upon a nest of centipedes and is eaten to the bone, the small town of Paia, Maui fights back, lead Afghanistan war vet, against the creepers who are terrorizing and taking over their town.

Mop Up

The residual effect of a toxic spill is discovered to the horror and indiscriminate termination of the clean-up crew.

Private Army

When the world's governments turn to private armies, the balance of power shifts and one man, running a corporate army, discovers a plot to overthrow these very same governments and must act to stop a global military coup d'etat.

The Aerialist

One woman, suffering from bi-polar disorder, decides to forgo medical treatment with help from a homeopathic doctor, so she can live her life without the debilitating effects of drugs much to the displeasure of her family.

RC Pilot

A lonely man in Minnesota builds and flies RC planes until he makes a new friend where he works who begins to show him other pleasures in life including beer and women.

The All-Seeing

In the future a religious cult has taken over the government but one man, tired of being told what to do, fights back to restore personal freedom and individuality.

ROMANTIC COMEDY

A sub-category of Comedy, Rom-Coms have become so popular and prevalent that some actresses are known strictly for their work in this genre. Meg Ryan made a career out of starring in Romantic Comedies beginning with *When Harry Met Sally*, then co-starring in two with Tom Hanks (*You've Got Mail* and *Sleepless in Seattle*).

A Romantic Comedy is any film where the main plot of the film is the male and female leads falling in love through a series of cinematic tropes, including the meet cute, the hidden secret, the reveal, the break-up, and the reconciliation.

Love Between the Sheets

A couple find they are better in bed than in a serious relationship and seek the help of professionals, friends and family to make their troubled relationship work.

Ruth

An aging, down-on-her-luck widow fortuitously meets a well-to-do man who desires to care for her but she must convince his kids it is a relationship divinely appointed.

A modern retelling of the Biblical story of Ruth.

Father Figure

More than just creative juices start flowing when a model and aspiring actress discovers that a handsome cab driver, who always seems to be there to pick her up, is also an aspiring screenwriter with a past.

For the Love of a Woman

When a young man who has grown up loving all women finally meets the one who may be his soul mate, he must change his playboy ways to win her heart.

The Packagers

After being hired as order fulfillment operators in the vast mega-structure of an Amazon.com warehouse, the staff becomes intertwined into each other's lives through love and hate.

It Happened More than One Night

After a one night stand keeps occurring between two unlikely lovers, their friends corroborate to keep them apart.

Do Not Remove Under Penalty of Law

A couple struggle with their relationship for years only to discover that it should be a crime to separate them as they are better together, even with all their difficulties, than apart.

The Perfect Day

After serendipitously meeting at a coffee shop in the morning a young man and women plan to create the perfect day together before they each must return to their respective lives.

The Perfect Ones

When a man explores the commonalities of what he considers the perfect woman, by dating and sleeping with them, he learns what really makes a woman perfect and discovers true love only after it may be too late.

Polar Opposites

A single traveling business man visits Hong Kong where he meets and falls in love with a younger colleague and he must overcome the generational and cultural differences—including her traditional father—to win her heart.

The Art of Sleeping

When a couple's marriage becomes too comfortable and boring, it takes a bit of imagination and dash of magic memories to refresh the feelings that each shared for the other to return them to their honeymoon phase.

Hot Leads

As an up and coming journalist and photographer partner to cover a breaking war story, sparks start flying, along with bullets, as the two discover each other along with the article.

Molecular

A man, genius for discovering revolutionary breakthroughs in molecular science, can barely tie his own shoes and has the social skills of a small child, but is forced to change when he meets a vivacious research assistant.

Flesh

Over the course of one night in one bar, one man and one woman meet for the first time and while tap dancing around their mutual attraction, wind up enacting the dynamics of male and female relationships.

That Shouldn't Matter

A couple must seek help from a professional counselor with unconventional methods, when they encounter difficulties in their twenty year marriage after the small things of life begin to take on greater significance than before.

Hey BAE

After meeting at a music festival, two youth, from different schools and with different friends, find it difficult to maintain a relationship when their friends try to keep them separated.

Show Me

After a wife is caught in a compromising position by her husband, he agrees to take her back only after she can show she has changed by completing ten steps to prove her love for him.

Immune

One man grows-up immune to the effects of love, due to being abandoned by his mother and father, and must face his lack of emotion and empathy when he encounters a women with a similar trait at their mutual friend's wedding.

Tripping over Angels

After publicly proclaiming that love is an illusion, one man has a spell cast on him where he finds love with every woman he meets, only to realize he risks losing the one woman who actually could be his soul-mate.

SCI-FI / FANTASY

To go where no man has gone before, into a galaxy far, far away — either into the future or into the long gone past — Science Fiction and Fantasy films often include many elements of other genres. These films can be dramatic (*The Lord of the Rings, Contact*), filled with action (*Elysium*), sometimes comedic (*Guardians of the Galaxy*), possibly horrific (*Aliens*), even Found Footage (*Cloverfield*).

Genetics

After a man discovers anomalies in his wife, he becomes entangled in a conspiracy and must expose the truth to save his family and his own life.

Islands

A young man on his tribal rite of passage sails into the vast ocean of the archipelago world only to be followed by the girl who loves him and he must protect them both from the dangers they encounter.

Oh No, I'm a Zombie!

After a young man is accidentally bitten by an infected monkey with a deadly virus, he becomes a zombie and must explain his new lifestyle to his parents, girlfriend and friends.

Out of Sync

After experimenting with mind-altering drugs while using a virtual reality application, a man finds his life out-of-sync with humanity and must correct it, only to find there is a much more sinister plot, arranged by the virtual reality programmer that he is a victim of.

1001001

After a special forces team of humans, cyborgs and robots, have their mission compromised on a hostile planet, they must use each of their individual skills to survive until a rescue team can arrive.

Crescent Orange

Earth has become a vast dust bowl until an alien race visits to save the planet and humans, who hold greater meaning in the universe than they know, only to face resistance from not only humans but other aliens.

Mega

Scientists studying the melting of the Arctic, discover eggs which have thawed and hatched, releasing monsters and the world's military must work together to fight them and save human kind.

Ship to Neuseus

When a mysterious, shape-shifting island-city rises from the ocean off the coast, a ship of raggedy volunteers, captained by drunk, is sent to investigate only to find themselves lost in a maze of fantasies and nightmares from which they must escape.

Domain Master

Legend of a crazy king hording great riches in a
vast dungeon system hidden in the mountains of
Gnordome, draws a thief, cleric, fighter and mage
who attempt to steal the treasure.

Polis

After the ice caps melt, the world's population
is forced to live on floating mega-cities, when
one woman discovers a government plot to thin
the population and she must race to stop the
genocide.

Archimedes Airship

One brilliant but emotionally damaged man invents an airship to live the rest of his days in the clouds until an accident forces him to land where he encounters a woman who needs his help and realizes he needs hers.

Undiscovered

Upon entering a secluded cenote in Central America, a team of scientists discover they have disturbed the feeding grounds of a prehistoric creature.

Drones

The skies are filled with malfunctioning,
autonomous killer drones and mankind has move
underground to survive until one teen decides to
fight back.

NOW SHOWING

THRILLER

The Thriller, or Suspense genre, uses tension and anxiety to create an emotional response in the viewer. While a Thriller can also be a Horror, to me, a true Thriller is dramatic, testing the expectations and anticipation of the viewer, creating surprise and adrenaline surges as the plot twists and turns.

Psychological, Crime, Erotic, Mystery, Techno, Legal, and Political are all common sub-genres of Thrillers along with Spy films. Alfred Hitchcock made Thrillers. Brian De Palma made Thrillers.

Thrillers have you on the edge of your seat and second guessing every character.

Body Paint

A young, aspiring model finds herself in an alluring but drug and sex filled world when she answers an ad for body paint model and is introduced to an intriguing, eccentric artist and his friends.

Travel Host

A couple discovers that the travel club they joined is killing its members and they must escape from their holiday before they become the next victims.

10cc

When a reporter discovers that doctors of one hospital believe they are above the law because of the prestige of their profession, he launches an investigation which puts his life in danger when he learns about cover-ups of medical malpractice and megalomaniacal behavior.

500mm

When police do not listen to a photographer reporting what appears a woman being thrown off a cliff which he inadvertently captures while shooting a swimsuit calendar, he investigates on his own only to become embroiled in a local scene of drugs, abduction and murder.

Origami

Unfolding over multiple generations and through
the stories of two apparently unrelated families,
a riddle to an age old secret worth millions
and which will shake the foundation of an
international company, can only be solved when
the grandchildren find the connection and work
together.

NOW SHOWING

TELEVISION

While television is more of a category than a genre, it has been given its own section in order to separate loglines that have been written specifically for television. A logline for TV has to establish a setting for an entire season of stories, as opposed to one complete story. I have noted the genre for each so you might better understand the tone I had in mind while writing these. Of course you may like an idea and think of a creative way to develop the story in an entirely different genre.

JetSet

Comedy

It's not all high-jinx at high altitude for the crew of luxury aircraft service, there is also sex, drugs and rock 'n' roll.

Animal House meets *The Great Gatsby* at 25,000 ft.

Tropo

Dramatic Comedy

When a mid-western man sets out to start a new life in the Caribbean he discovers that life owning and operating a bar is not as simple as he had hoped and imagined.

On Property

Dramatic Comedy

Customer service is key for the staff of a five star resort on Maui who must deal with crazy customer requests, native traditions, outrageous Hollywood actor antics and more.

The Prophet of Park St.

Comedy

Comic books, collector's cards, collectibles and sage wisdom are all offered to the group of pre-teen customers—struggling with identity issues and puberty—by the owners of a garage based shop.
The Way Way Back at a comic con.

Second Chance

Drama

Chance Andrews dies only to be sent back to life with the mandate to help others deal with their own personal struggles.

Favor

Drama

One man helps people solve their problems by calling in favors from the others he has helped throughout the years and once a person's problem is solved, they now owe a favor.

Psyops

Military Drama

Counter terrorist operators use mind tricks and manipulation instead of guns and bombs to win battles of hearts and minds.

YA

Dramatic Comedy

After hormones kick in, a group of 14 and 15 year olds wind a path through the mine field of romance, love, sex and pimples with the aid of a cool counselor who they meet each week in group sessions.

I f some films are described literally, and with a
tongue firmly placed in cheek, the resulting
logline seems a bit skewed. That's what makes this
exercise in absurdity so much fun.

What follows are classic, and/or, popular films
from recent years with honest, but somewhat
twisted perspective loglines.

Can you guess the film for which the logline is
written? Answers are provide at the end of the
section.

A diminutive recluse is coerced by a mysterious older man into following thirteen burly strangers into the wilderness with promises of riches but also possible dismemberment and incineration on an unexpected adventure.

A hapless town sheriff, a smart-ass scientist and a booze soaked, war veteran, ship captain discover they need a bigger boat to save their lives from the world's largest psychopathic man-eater.

When a man with a history of dressing as a bat meets a beautiful woman dressed as a cat, they must team up to battle a psychotic, unintelligible man to prevent a nuclear explosion before they can explore their love for each other.

When a covert operative discovers that the surrogate mother he works for has dark secrets to hide he must decide between partnering with an effeminate co-worker to expose the truth or remain loyal and save her and the government he works for.

When an orphaned alien with delusions of
grandeur tries to take over Earth, five anti-social
super human vigilantes are forced to work out
their differences and cooperate to stop the alien
invasion.

An antagonistic teenage girl, with authority issues,
volunteers to fight to the death against other
teenagers including the boy who secretly loves her
for the entertainment of a country.

An adult man struggles to maintain his relationship with the woman he loves with the help of his long-time friend, a pot smoking, hooker chasing, talking teddy bear.

A teenage boy, with father issues explores his masculinity by wearing spandex and swinging through the city, only to face a giant lizard-man bent on perfecting human evolution with plans for world domination.

One woman's obsession with a reclusive Middle Eastern man with bad social skills leads to a world-wide military manhunt.

Beginning at the top of page 148, the films described include:

The Hobbit
Jaws
The Dark Knight Rises
Skyfall
The Avengers
The Hunger Games
Ted
The Amazing Spider-Man
Zero Dark Thirty